My Book of Snakes

of

Snakes

Willie Ortiz

Danger

Venomous

Reptiles

Ahead

Venomous snakes are found throughout many regions of the world and are a threat to public health, especially in the rural tropics where they are most abundant. Out of more than 3000 species of snakes in the world, some 600 are venomous and over 200 are medically important.

African Bush Viper

Venomous

They live in Tanzania and are expert climbers sometimes found high in the brush.

Highly variable in color, eats rodents, lizards and frogs.

There is **NO** antivenom for this toxic little guy.

Lives in Angola, Namibia and South Africa. This small python is often called a dwarf python and is rare in captive collections. It can grow to about six feet long. This snake's habitat is littered with landmines from civil war in Angola and, because of this, collectors are reluctant to go there to collect the snakes. This snake feeds on small mammals and birds. This snake is closely related to the Ball Python.

Black Mamba

Venomous

The Black Mamba is Africa's largest venomous snake.
They feed primarily on small mammals and ground dwelling birds.
The Black Mamba is one of the world's most dangerous snakes.
They can inject up to ten lethal doses of venom in a single bite!

Distinguishable from other arboreal snakes by very large eyes.

Chameleons are their usual diet, but they will sometimes eat birds and frogs.

Venom is an extremely toxic hemotoxin that has coagulopathic properties, which cause hemorrhaging from the gums, nose, and other orifices, even scratches.

This snake has the most toxic venom of all the cobras. They live in South Africa, parts of Botswana and Namibia.

They range in color from black, brown, yellow, or sometimes speckled.

They are primarily terrestrial, although they will raid birds' nests.

Egyptian Cobra

Venomous

They live in North Africa and the Middle East.

Their diet consists of amphibians, birds, and small mammals.

The Egyptian Cobra is one of the largest and most common cobras in Africa. Cobras have specialized muscles and ribs in their neck that flare out when they are threatened. They will raise up, spread their hood, and hiss loudly to scare off the threat.

Venomous

They live in Western Africa. Gaboon Vipers can weigh up to 40 pounds, making them one of the heaviest snakes in Africa. Do not get fooled though, because they are very fast!

These Vipers eat small mammals, birds, frogs, and toads.

They are ambush predators that will hide in leaves on the forest floor to ambush their victims.

This snake lives Southward from Tanzania to Eastern Zimbabwe and Coastal Natal in South Africa.

The Green Mamba is the smallest of the family of Mambas.

This species, although normally arboreal, occasionally descends to the ground to forage. If startled, it will ascend the nearest tree and escape through the foliage.

Green Mambas are extremely venomous.

The Puff Adder is a venomous viper found in the African savannah and grasslands.

The species is the most common and widespread snake in the continent. The Adder is the number one cause of snake bites in Africa.

When the Adder is disturbed, the snake will coil into a defensive S-shaped posture and hiss loudly to scare off the intruder.

Puff Adders can have up to 60 babies at one time.

The western green mamba's venom is like those of other members of the mamba family but differs from others in toxicity and the composition of the toxins. The venom consists mostly of both pre- and post-synaptic neurotoxins, cardiotoxins, and fasciculins. The toxicity of their venom varies tremendously depending on various factors including diet, geographical location, age, and other factors.

Black racer

Non - Venomous

The Black Racer is found throughout mainland Florida and the Keys. The Black Racer is fast moving and can climb and swim very well. When discovered, the racer will flee for shelter, relying on its speed and agility to avoid capture. However, when cornered, its only defense is to strike. Its bite is harmless, but it has needle-sharp teeth that can cause bleeding. When annoyed, it may rapidly vibrate its tail in the leaf litter, producing a buzzing sound.

Anaconda

Non - Venomous

Anacondas can stay under water for 10 minutes before it comes to the surface to grab some air.
Their whole body stays submerged except for their nostrils, which are on their head. They eat fish, turtles, caimans, capybaras, pigs, jaguars, and deer.
They eat 40 pounds of food a day.

Brown water snake

Non - Venomous

The Brown Water Snakes are often mistaken with poisonous cottonmouths. Brown Water Snakes eat fish, frogs, earthworms, small snakes, and rodents. Females are not able to hunt during pregnancy due to extra weight and therefore store reserves well in advance for the duration of their pregnancy. They don't like to eat catfish because their spines cause them a lot of pain. If they eat a catfish, the spine of a catfish will protrude from their body. The spine breaks away after some time and the wound will heal.

Canebreak/Timber Rattlesnake

Venomous

Snake of the S. E. Coastal plain, including North Florida, with his upland brother known as the Timber Rattlesnake.

Once abundant in the Eastern U.S., this snake has been exterminated in many parts of its former range.

Florida Resident

Coral Snake

Venomous

Coral Snakes are closely related to Cobras, Mambas, and Sea Snakes.
They have the most toxic venom of any North American Snake.
The Coral Snake can be recognized by the rhyme "Red to yellow kill a fellow."
They live in the coastal plain of the U.S., including all of Florida.

Corn/Red Ratsnake

Non - Venomous

Vibrant color and docile temperament make the Corn snake a captive.
Corn snakes belong to the family of snakes known as constrictors. These snakes wrap their body around the victim and squeeze it until it dies of suffocation. Corn snakes are carnivores (meat eaters).

Eastern Diamondback Rattlesnake

Venomous

They are the largest venomous snake in North America.

They eat small mammals.

Their tail can rattle at sixty cycles per second.

They live on the coastal plain of the South East U.S., including all of Florida.

Fer de Lance

Venomous

This snake is also called "Lance Head."

It also has a virulent venom that has caused many human fatalities.

This snake is very common in forested areas of Central and South America.

Cottonmouths are often confused with the Non – Venomous Brown Water Snake.

Cottonmouths are distinguishable by their vertical pupils and facial pit. Water snakes have round pupils and no facial pit.

They eat fish, frogs, rodents, lizards, birds, and small snakes.

They are called Cottonmouths because their mouth is white inside, so when they open their mouth you see all white - like cotton.

Florida Kingsnake

Non - Venomous

They are found in Central and Southern Florida.

They eat snakes, lizards, frogs, rodents, turtle eggs, birds, and bird eggs.

Kingsnakes are valuable in keeping down rodent populations especially near human settlements.

Florida Pine Snake

Non - Venomous

Florida Pine snakes spend most of their time in gopher tortoise holes.

They are protected by Florida law.

They eat pocket gophers, small mammals, lizards, and eggs.

Florida Ringneck Snake

Non - Venomous

They live all over the United States, not just in Florida. They can be found as high up as Canada and into central Mexico.

The snake has teeth and is also slightly venomous, though not to humans.

They are nocturnal and they do not cause much human problems as it does not come out of hiding unless disturbed.

Florida Watersnake

Non - Venomous

They live in the South Eastern United States and all of Florida.

They eat fish, frogs, tadpoles, amphibians, and other invertebrates.

They are often confused with the venomous Cottonmouth and needlessly killed because of this resemblance.

Mojave Rattlesnake

Venomous

This snake has an extremely toxic venom.

In some areas of its range the venom contains a potent neurotoxin.

This snake is shy and reclusive, but if molested it will aggressively protect itself.

This snake lives in the Southwestern United States.

Pygmy Rattlesnake

Venomous

This little snake accounts for the majority of venomous snake bites in Florida.

Due to its small size and low venom yield, pygmy bites are almost never fatal!

They live in all peninsular Florida and parts of the South Eastern United States.

Red Pygmy Rattlesnake

Venomous

This little snake is very desirable among collectors and is now protected because of over collecting.

This snake lives in the Southeastern United States.

Pygmies show considerable variation in venom over their range, lifetime, and diet.

This snake lives in extreme Southwestern Texas, small sections of Arizona, New Mexico, and Northern Mexico.

Their venom is very toxic and variable through their range.

This snake is varies tremendously in color depending on where you find him.

They live in the Coastal plain of the Southeastern United States.

Copperhead bites are serious and very painful but almost never fatal.

The beautiful copper color on their head gives the snake its name.

Southern Pacific Rattlesnake

Venomous

They live in Southern California into the Baja Peninsula.

This dangerous snake is usually featured on Discovery's Venom ER.

Current antivenom does a poor job of neutralizing this snake's venom.

This snake is a major cause of snake bites in Southern California.

Western diamondback Rattlesnake

Venomous

They live throughout the American Southwest and Northern Mexico.

Large venom volume and the snake being very nervous makes it very dangerous.

Aruba Island Rattlesnake

Venomous

Aruba Island Rattlesnakes are endangered because of logging, agriculture, and development.

They live on Aruba Island off the coast of Venezuela.

They eat small rodents, lizards, and birds.

There are five species of jumping vipers native to Mexico and Central America.

They eat lizards, rodents, and frogs.

They like to hide under fallen logs and leaves, which makes it hard to see them.

Emerald Tree Boa

Non - Venomous

They are mostly nocturnal and spend most of the day coiled up on a tree branch with their head at center of their body.

The Boas are viviparous, meaning the embryos develop internally. The babies are born able to climb and fend for themselves. They require no maternal care.

They eat mammals, birds, lizards, and frogs.

Mexican Lance Headed Rattlesnake

Venomous

They live in Mexico.

They eat amphibians, reptiles, insects, and small mammals.

The Rattlesnake's rattle comes from a series of interlocking keratin rings that create a hissing sound when vibrated. Another ring is added each time the snake sheds its skin.

Ornate Cantil

Venomous

They live in Mexico and Central America.

The cantil has the largest fangs in proportion to its body size of any Agkistrodon family, which includes the copperhead and the cottonmouth.

They eat amphibians, birds, mammals, and reptiles.

They live in Brazil, Bolivia, Paraguay, and Uruguay.

They have a highly toxic venom with high concentrations of neurotoxins.

Victims bitten by this snake must be treated quickly!

Yellow Eyelash Viper

Venomous

They live in central and South America.

These are arboreal snakes, meaning they spend their lives in trees, palms, shrubs, and vines. They also prefer to stay near a permanent water source.

Costa Rican Green Pit Viper

Venomous

Vipers are from a large family of snakes whose scientific name is Viperidae. They are found all over the world, with the exceptions of Antarctica, Australia, New Zealand, Madagascar, north of the Arctic Circle, and island clusters like Hawaii.

The family Viperidae includes adders, pit vipers (like rattlesnakes, cottonmouths and copperheads), the Gaboon viper, green vipers, and horned vipers.

Boa Constrictor

Non - Venomous

Some Boas have heat-sensitive scales around their mouths that help them find prey in the dark.

They eat birds, lizards, frogs and small mammals, monkeys, pigs, and deer.

Boa Constrictors along with the Reticulated Python and Anaconda are one of the largest snakes in the world.

Asian Monacled Cobra

Venomous

The Asian Monacled Cobra lives in South Asia and Southeast Asia.
They eat small mammals and snakes.
The monacled cobra's venom is one of the fastest acting venoms in the world. Its venom's potency depends on where the snake is found.
The venom can cause death within an hour of the bite. The neurotoxins in its venom lead to drowsiness, neurological problems, and muscle issues.

They are the world's largest venomous snake and can grow up to 18 feet long.
They live in India, South East Asia, Malay Peninsula, Indonesia, and the Philippines.
They eat mostly snake and lizards.
They inject large volumes of highly toxic venom.
They are the only snake known to make a nest to lay their eggs.

New Guinea Taipan

Venomous

They live in Southern New Guinea.

They eat birds, rodents, and small mammals.

It is estimated that venom from a single bite from a Taipan could kill 125,000 mice!

Sri Lankan Pit Viper

Venomous

They live in Sri Lanka.

They eat small mammals, lizards, frogs, and birds.

Sri Lanka is mostly an agricultural country, resulting in a large number of people being bitten while picking tea leaves, weeding, and clearing lands.

They live in sections of New Guinea, The Northern coast, and a small area of Central Australia.

They are the largest of Australia's venomous snakes, reaching 7 feet long.

They are often considered the world's most dangerous snake.

Taipans typically bite higher than other snakes, biting the calf.

Jungle Carpet Python

Non - Venomous

They live in Northern Australia.

They eat small mammals, birds, and reptiles.

They have heat sensing pits lining their upper lip to find prey and to hide from predators.

Boas and Pythons have three or more of these pits while Vipers have only one large pit.

The End

About the Author

Willie Ortiz is an avid wildlife, nature, and travel photographer. He has traveled extensively across Asia, Europe, and the Americas to view and photograph animals in their natural habitat. When the natural habitat is almost impossible, Willie is a patron of animal rehabilitation and education centers. Animals of Belize, Willie's first book truly shows the passion he has for protecting wildlife through education. Willie's photography reflects his love of nature and expresses a unique perspective of history, nature, and the world around us. Willie's catalog of books includes children's educational, travel, nature, and history themes. Willie Ortiz is originally from the Bronx and currently resides on the Treasure Coast of Florida.